Super Safari

Level 1

Workbook

Herbert Puchta   Günter Gerngross   Peter Lewis-Jones

CAMBRIDGE
UNIVERSITY PRESS

CAMBRIDGE
UNIVERSITY PRESS

University Printing House, Cambridge CB2 8BS, United Kingdom

One Liberty Plaza, 20th Floor, New York, NY 10006, USA

477 Williamstown Road, Port Melbourne, VC 3207, Australia

314–321, 3rd Floor, Plot 3, Splendor Forum, Jasola District Centre, New Delhi – 110025, India

79 Anson Road, #06–04/06, Singapore 079906

Cambridge University Press is part of the University of Cambridge.

It furthers the University's mission by disseminating knowledge in the pursuit of education, learning, and research at the highest international levels of excellence.

www.cambridge.org
Information on this title: www.cambridge.org/9781107481787

© Cambridge University Press 2015

First published 2015

22

Printed in Great Britain by CPI Group (UK) Ltd, Croydon CR0 4YY

A catalogue record for this publication is available from the British Library

ISBN 978-1-107-48178-7 Workbook Level 1
ISBN 978-1-107-48177-0 Student's Book with DVD-ROM Level 1
ISBN 978-1-107-48180-0 Teacher's Book Level 1
ISBN 978-1-107-48186-2 Teacher's DVD Level 1
ISBN 978-1-107-48181-7 Class Audio CDs Level 1
ISBN 978-1-107-47679-0 Flashcards Level 1
ISBN 978-1-107-48184-8 Presentation Plus DVD-ROM Level 1
ISBN 978-1-107-47729-2 Posters Level 1
ISBN 978-1-107-47732-2 Puppet

Additional resources for this publication at www.cambridge.org/supersafari/ame

Super Safari Level 1 Workbook

Hello!

1 Look and trace. Say the names.

Gina, Polly, Leo, Mike

2 Draw yourself. Say the sentence.

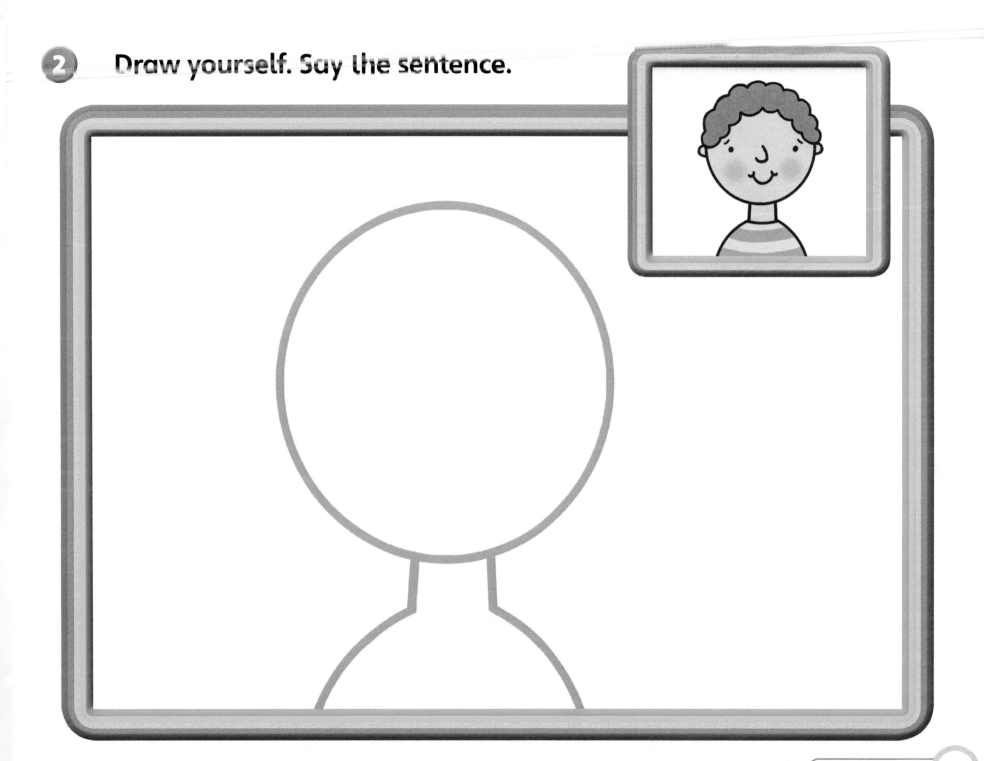

Hello! I'm (Jo).   5

3 CD1 05 **Listen and circle.**

④ Say the names. Color the circles.

1

2

3

4

1 My class

1 Look and match. Say the words.

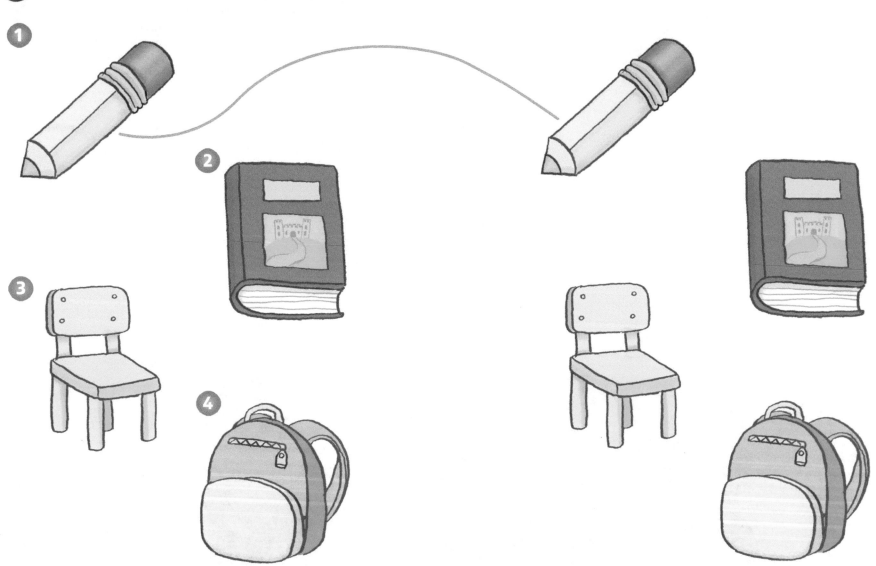

bag, pencil, book, chair

2 CD1 10 **Listen and connect the dots. Say the sentence.**

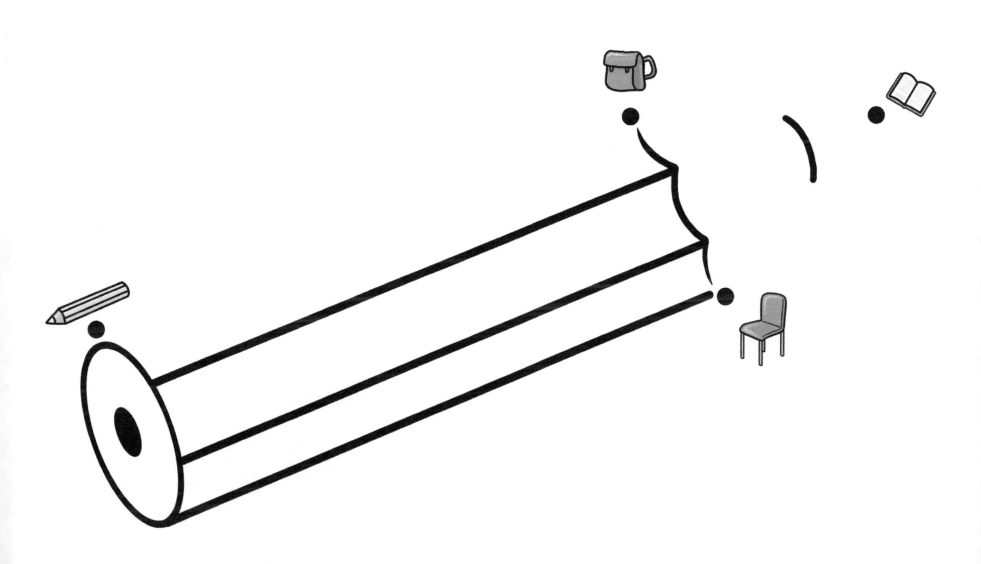

Look! It's my (pencil). 9

3 CD1 12 **Listen and circle.**

4 Follow the path.

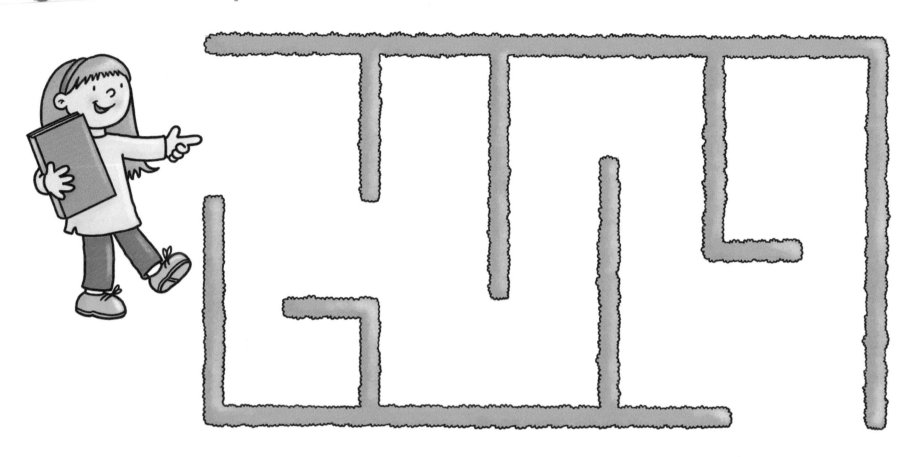

5 Listen and color the correct circle.

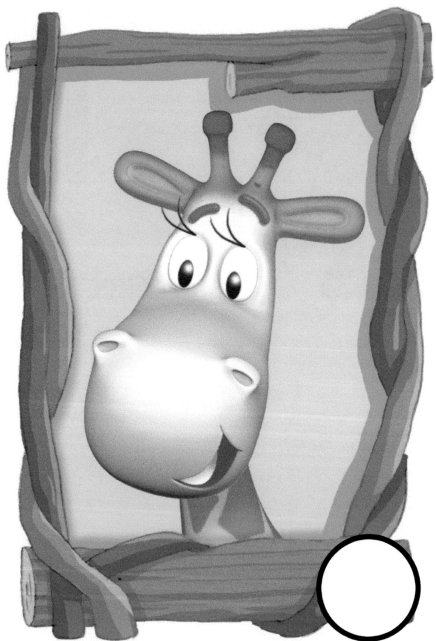

6 **Complete the face (☺). Color the picture.**

7 Make a model of yourself.

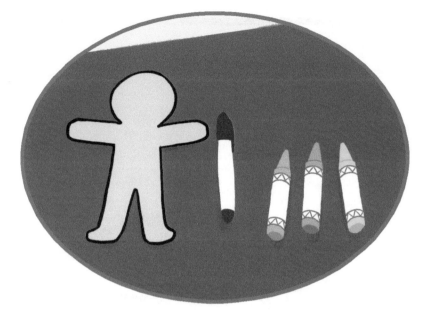

Say the words. Color the circles.

1

2

3

4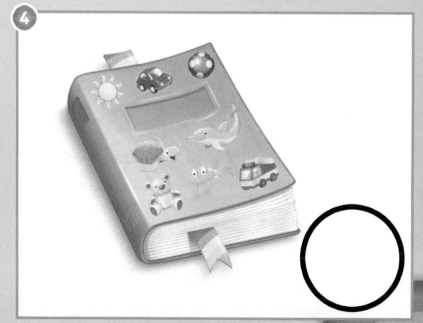

2 My colors

Look and color. Say the colors.

red, blue, green, yellow

2 Look and color. Say the sentences.

It's (red).

3 CD1 24 **Listen and circle.**

4 CD1 Listen again and color.

5 **Listen and color the correct circle.**

6 Complete the face (☺). Color the picture.

7 Make a mixed-color painting.

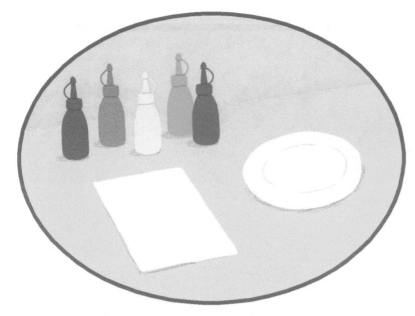

8 Say the colors. Color the circles.

1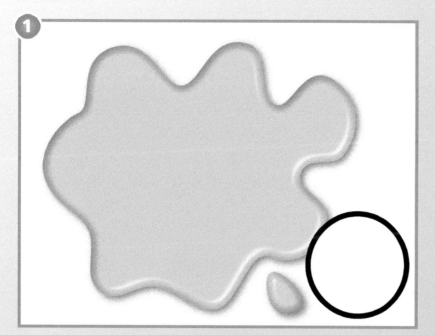

2

3

4

3 My family

1 **Look and circle the different picture. Say the words.**

dad, mom, brother, sister

2 Draw a family member. Say the sentence.

3 ^{CD1} **Listen and circle.**

4 Listen and match.

1

2

5 Listen and color the correct circle.

6 Complete the face (🙂). Color the picture.

7 Make a rocking chicken.

8 Say the words. Color the circles.

1

2

3

4

4 My toys

ball, car, puzzle, doll

2 Draw a toy. Say the sentence.

I have a (ball).

3 CD1 50 Listen and circle.

4 CD1 53 Listen again. Trace and color.

5 CD1 55 Listen and color the correct circle.

6 Complete the face (☺). Color the picture.

7 Make a big toy and a small toy.

8 Say the toys. Color the circles.

1

2

3

4

5 My numbers

1 Listen and color. Say the numbers.

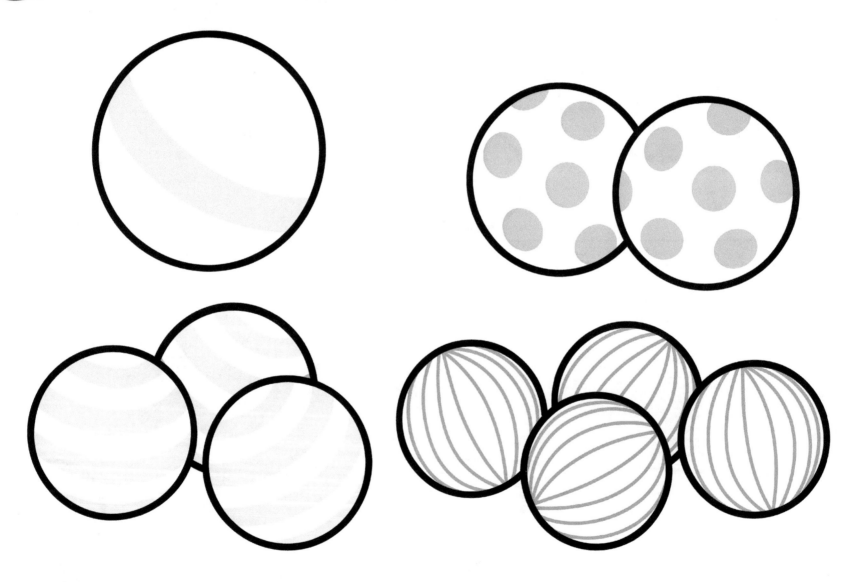

2 **Look and circle. Say the sentences.**

4 **Listen again and color.**

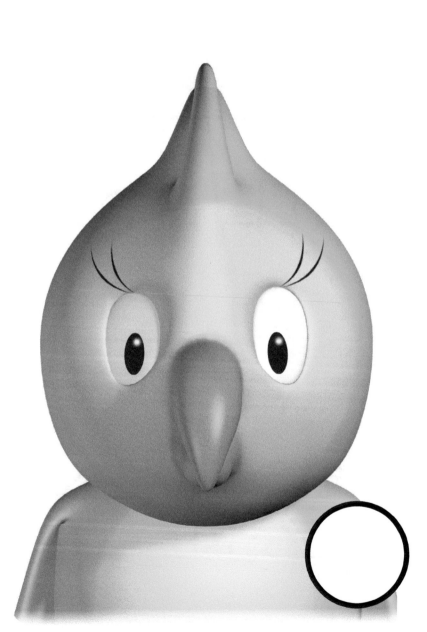

Complete the face (☺). Color the picture.

7 **Make a number train.**

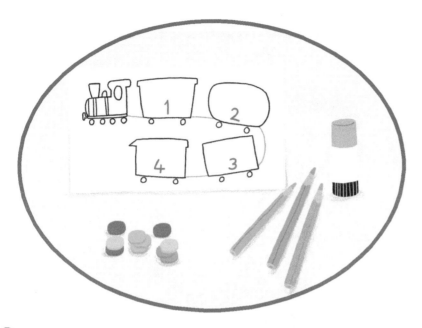

8 Say the numbers. Color the circles.

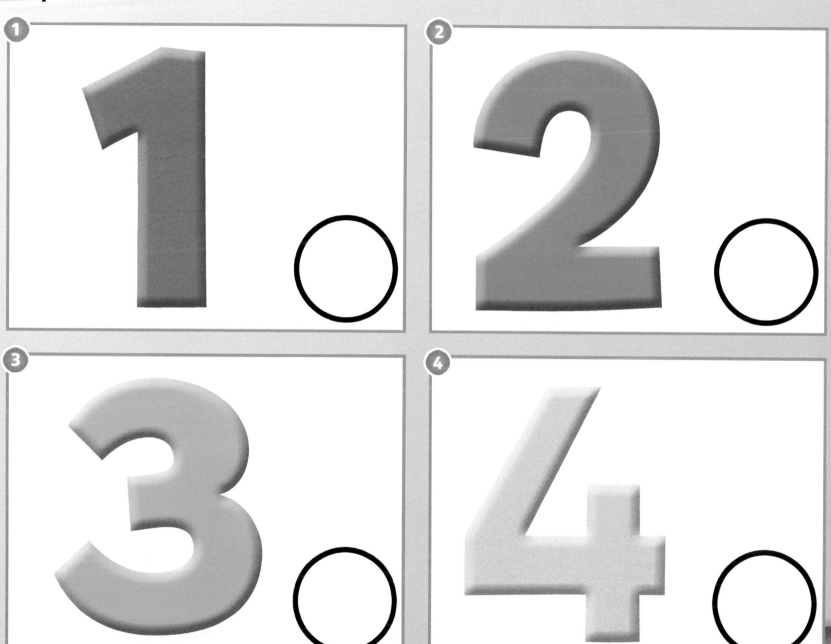

6 My pets

1 **Look and circle the different pictures. Say the pets.**

1

2

3

bird, rabbit, fish, cat

2 CD2 10 Listen and connect the dots. Say the sentence.

Listen and circle.

Total physical response

6 Complete the face (☺). Color the picture.

7 **Make a handprint bird.**

Say the pets. Color the circles.

1

2

3

4

7 My food

1 **Look and match. Say the food.**

pasta, salad, rice, cake

2 **Draw something you like. Say the sentence.**

I like (salad).

Listen and circle.

1

2

4 Follow the path.

5 CD2 36 Listen and color the correct circles.

1

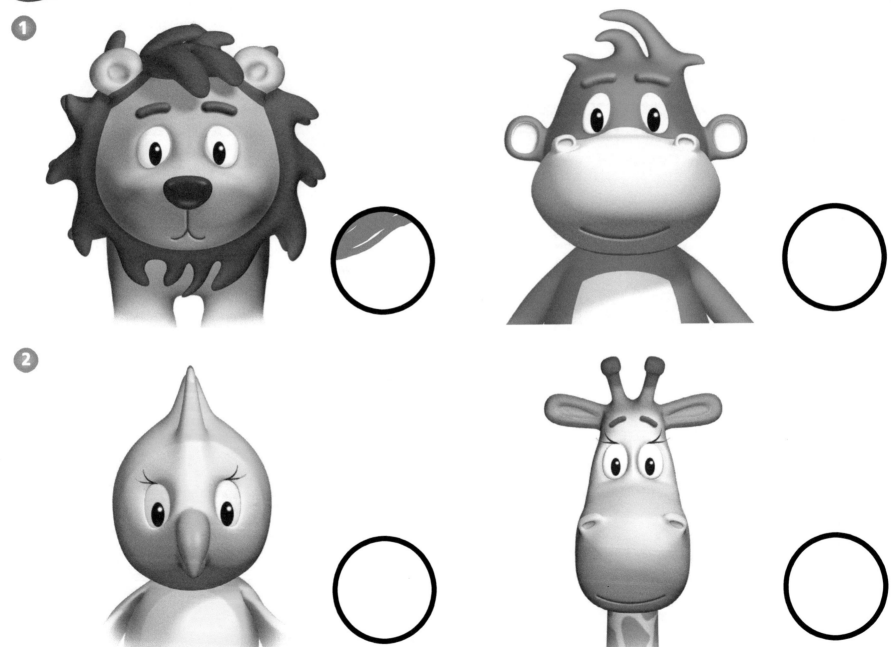

2

6 Complete the face (☺). Color the picture.

7 **Make a pasta fish.**

8 **Say the food. Color the circles.**

1

○

2

○

3

○

4

○

1 Look and circle. Say the clothes.

T-shirt, pants, dress, shoes

2 CD2 **Listen and cross out (✗) the "don't likes". Say the sentences.**

I don't like (the purple hat). **65**

Listen and circle.

1

2

4 **Look and match the children with their clothes.**

1

2

5 Listen and color the correct circles.

CD2 49

1

2

6 Complete the face (:)). Color the picture.

7 Make a hat.

8 Say the clothes. Color the circles.

1

◯

2

◯

3

◯

4

◯

9 My park

1 CD2 53 **Listen and color. Say the words.**

1

2

3

4

slide, merry-go-round, seesaw, swing

2 Listen and connect the dots. Say the sentence.

The (slide)'s fun.

Listen and circle.

Total physical response

4 Follow the path and count the swings.

5 **CD2** **62** Listen and color the correct circles.

1

2

6 Complete the face (☺). Color the picture.

7 Make a shapes cat.

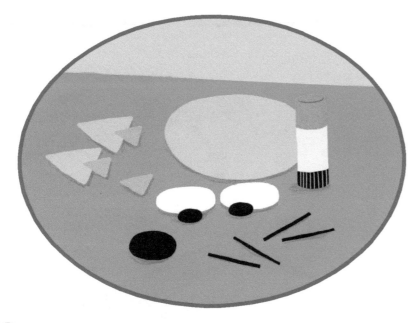

8 **Say the words. Color the circles.**

1

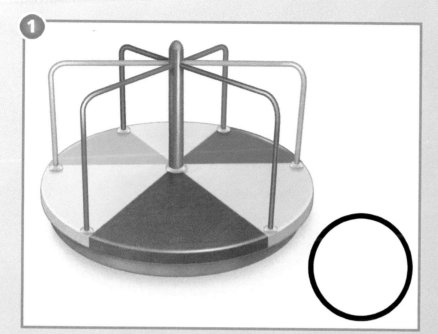

2

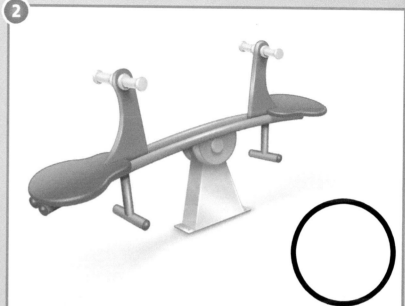

3

4

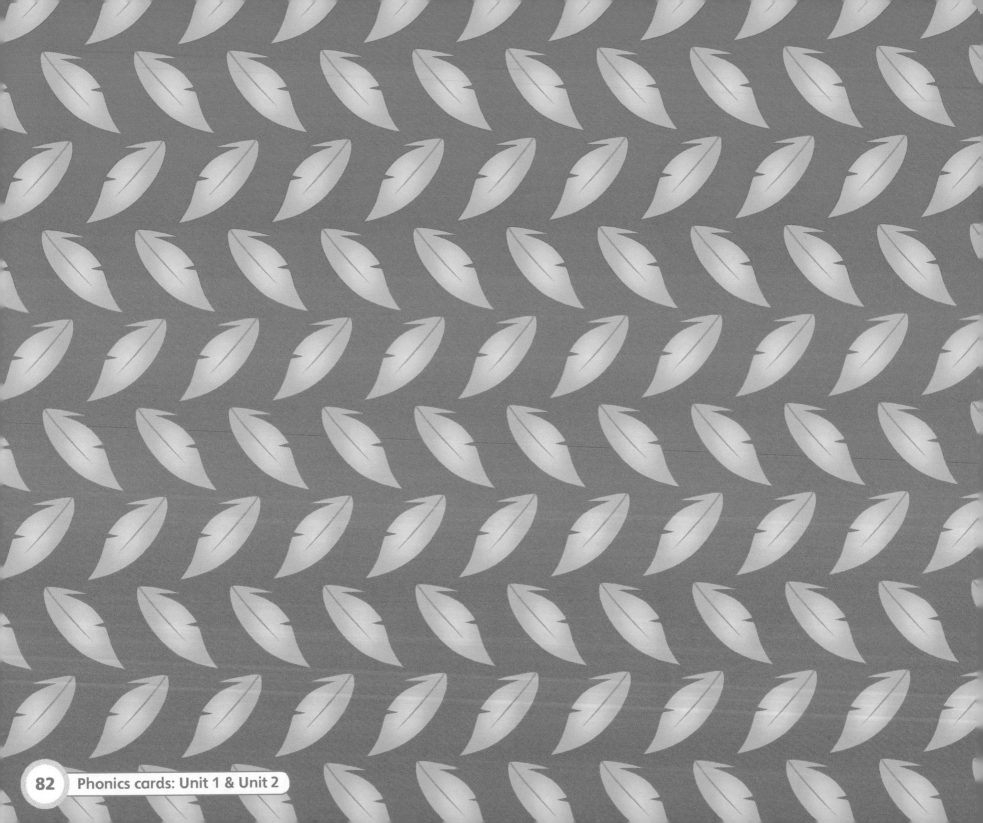

t

e

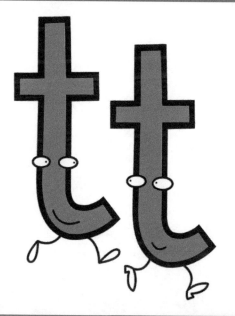

Phonics cards: Unit 7 & Unit 8

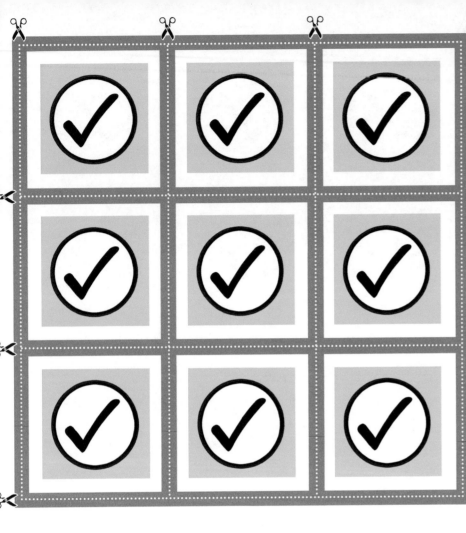

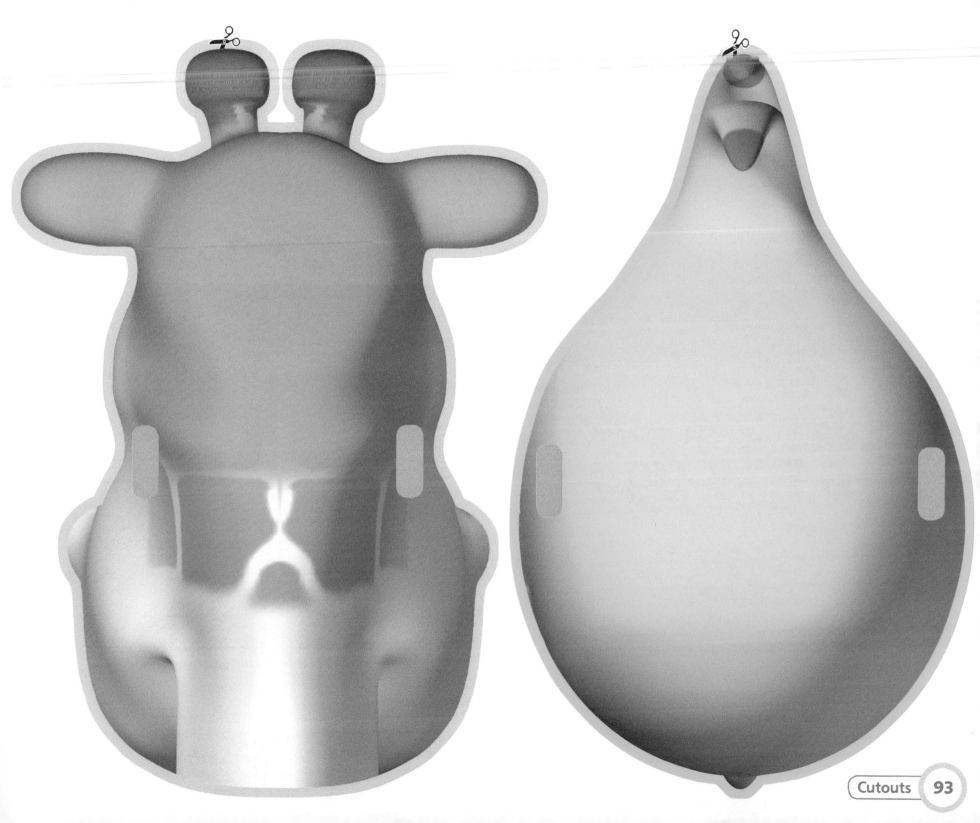

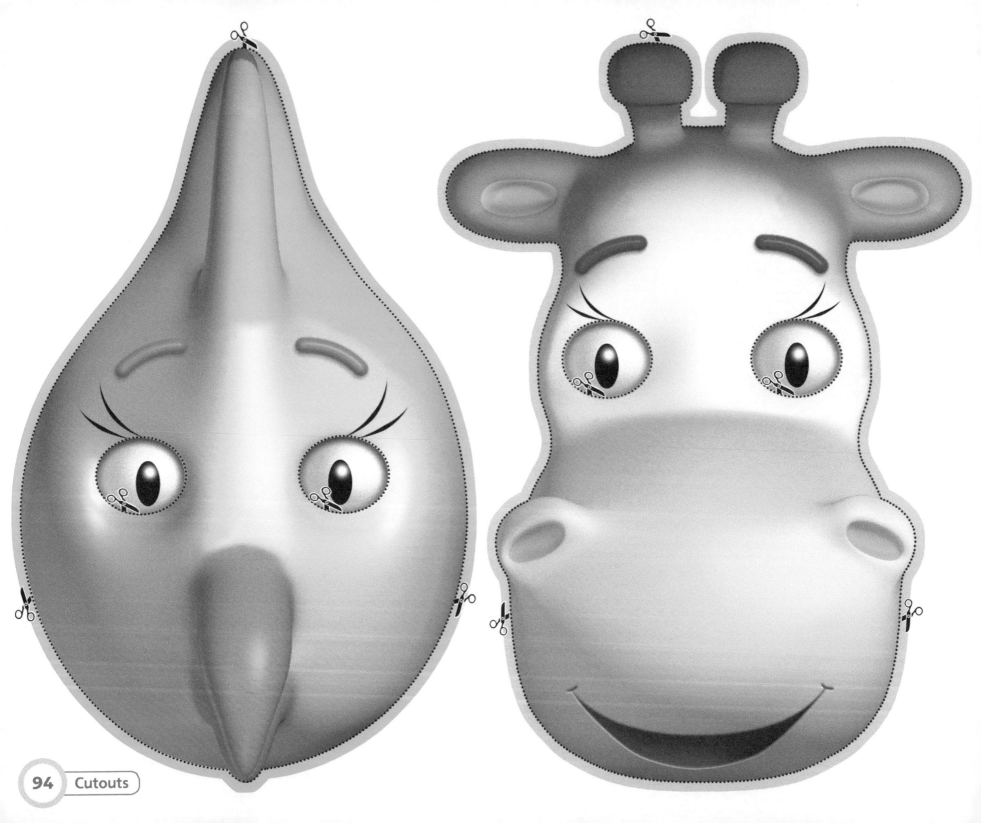

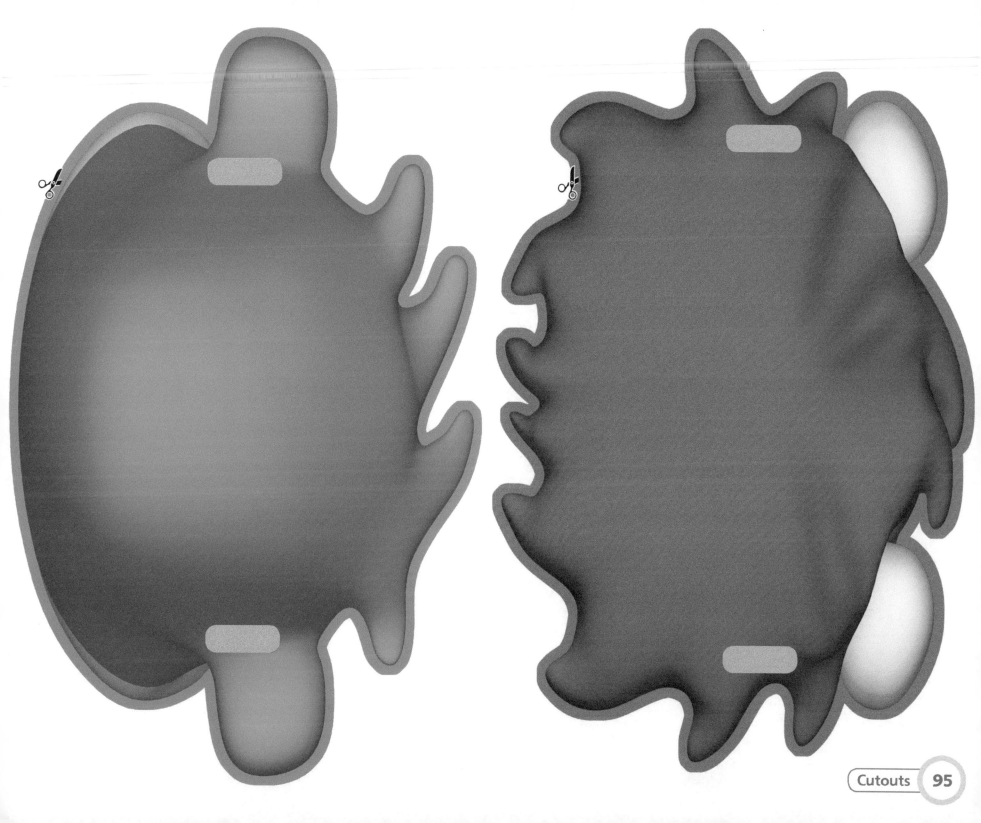

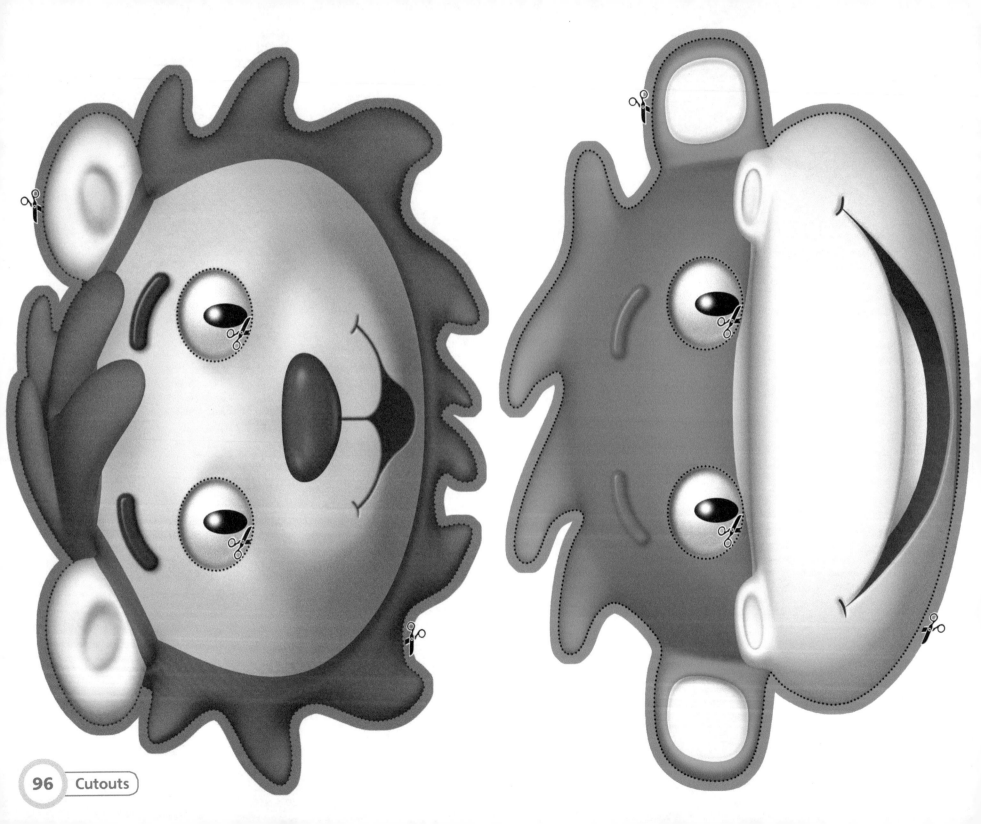